OUTCRY

FROM

THE

INFERNO

Atomic

Bomb

Tanka

Anthology

To Charlotte
with my best wishes

Jim Nebano
Sept 19, 1995

Also by Jiro Nakano

Poets Behind Barbed Wire
(Bamboo Ridge Press, 1983)

OUTCRY FROM THE INFERNO

Atomic Bomb Tanka Anthology

edited
and
translated
by
Jiro
Nakano

This is a special double issue of *Bamboo Ridge, The Hawaii Writers Quarterly*, issues #67 and #68 (Summer/Fall 1995), ISSN 0733-0308.

ISBN 0-910043-38-8
Published by Bamboo Ridge Press
Copyright 1995 Jiro Nakano
All rights reserved.
Printed in the United States.
Cover art by Toshi Maruki. Used with
    permission of the artist.
Book design: Susanne Yuu.
Calligraphy: Rev. Shohei Hatta
Typesetting and production: Wayne
    Kawamoto.

Bamboo Ridge Press is a non-profit, tax-exempt organization formed to foster the appreciation, understanding, and creation of literary, visual, audio-visual and performing arts by and about Hawaii's people. Your tax-deductible contributions are welcomed. Bamboo Ridge is supported, in part, by grants from the State Foundation on Culture and the Arts (SFCA). The SFCA is funded by appropriations from the Hawai'i State Legislature and by grants from the National Endowment for the Arts, a Federal agency. Bamboo Ridge Press is a member of the Council of Literary Magazines and Presses (CLMP).

BAMBOO RIDGE PRESS
P. O. BOX 61781
HONOLULU, HAWAI'I 96839-1781
(808) 599-4823

99 98 97 96 95   1 2 3 4 5 6

Library of Congress Cataloging-in-Publication Data

Outcry from the inferno, atomic bomb tanka anthology
    / edited and translated by Jiro Nakano.
            p.   cm.
    In English and Japanese.
    Includes bibliographical references.
    ISBN 0-910043-38-8 : $10.00
    1. Waka. 2. Japanese poetry—Shōwa period,
1926–1989. 3. Atomic bomb victims—Poetry.
4.Hiroshima-shi (Japan)—History—Bombardment,
1945—Poetry. 5.Nagasaki-shi (Japan)—History—
Bombardment, 1945—Poetry.   6. Waka—
Translations into English. 7. Japanese poetry—
Shōwa period, 1926–1989—Translations into
English. I. Nakano, Jiro.
PL758.875.H52096   1995   95-23262
                                            CIP

CONTENTS

FOREWORD

About four years ago, Dr. Nakano wrote to
me saying he would like to select the best 100
tanka about the atomic bombing and translate
them into English. After I received his letter, I
provided him with several thousand tanka poems
written by the atomic bomb victims and informa-
tion about each poet. On November 20, 1994, he
visited my house in Hiroshima, showed me the
manuscript of the anthology and asked me to
review the selected poems. As I glanced through
it, I was amazed to see the quality of the tanka
selected by Dr. Nakano. I have eagerly awaited
completion of his project.

In August 1945, I was severely injured by
the atomic bombing in Hiroshima and hovered
between life and death for about six months.
Thereafter, I barely survived though I developed
two types of cancers presumably because of
radiation. I have written a large number of tanka
on the atomic bombing and published five tanka
collections. I also compiled and edited several
thousand tanka and published two anthologies,
Kashū Hiroshima (Tanka Anthology: Hiroshima)

and *Hankaku-shuka-hyakuzetsu* (Anti-nuclear Tanka Anthology). Thus, I have come to believe that writing and reading atomic bomb tanka are my karma and life-long work.

The tanka compiled by Dr. Nakano in this anthology, were written by the *hibakusha* (survivors of the bombing), by leading tanka poets in Japan such as Yoshimi Kondo, and by literary scholars such as Dr. Takashi Nagai who was a victim of the atomic bombing in Nagasaki and the author of *The Bell of Nagasaki*. Many other excellent anti-nuclear tanka, however, were written by ordinary housewives such as Mrs. Momoyo Ishii.

I admired Dr. Nakano's literary sense in selecting these superb tanka from many thousands. In the past fifty years after the end of World War II, I have read at least 50,000 tanka related to the atomic bombing. I am very happy to learn that Dr. Nakano translated these poems and is publishing this anthology for a large number of readers in the United States and Europe. Many have protested that nuclear proliferation in the world eventually would result in the annihila-

tion of mankind from the earth. It is very impor-
tant for people to read these tanka and to realize
that cessation of atomic weapons is sine-qua-non
for preservation of world peace.

Seishi Toyota
May 20, 1995
Hiroshima

*Seishi Toyota is one of the foremost tanka poets in
Japan, and President of the Kagen Tanka Society, and
the editor of the tanka magazine Kagen.*

ACKNOWLEDGMENTS

I am deeply thankful to master tanka poet
and the editor of the tanka poem magazine, *Kaen*
(Flame), Mr. Seishi Toyota, for his kindness in
permitting me to use poems from his anthologies
of the atomic bombing *Kashū Hiroshima* and
Hankaku-shuka-hyakuzetsu. He also gave me
generous advice in publishing this book and in
writing the foreword.

I also wish to express my sincere appre-
ciation to my two friends and poets, Frances
Kakugawa and Eric Chock of Honolulu, for reading
the poems and for giving me their invaluable
criticism. I also acknowledge Gail Harada, Rev.
Shohei Hatta, Wayne Kawamoto, Joy Kobayashi,
Thomas Kondo, Darrell H.Y. Lum, and Susanne
Yuu for their efforts in the production of this book.

Finally, I will not forget the affections of
my wife, Hisako, and my daughter, Serene, for
their continual encouragement and assistance in
the publication of this anthology.

INTRODUCTION

Nearly a half century has passed since the fatal morning of August 6, 1945, when the first atomic bomb was dropped in Hiroshima by a B-12 bomber called "Enola Gay." Instantly, it turned the peaceful city into an inferno. It killed more than twenty thousand people and left thirty thousand more homeless. Subsequently, survivors known as *hibakusha* succumbed to cancer and leukemia induced by radiation.

President Harry S. Truman and other American politicians insisted that the dropping of the atomic bomb was necessary for the United States to expedite the end of the war and to save the lives of American soldiers in the planned invasion of Honshu, Japan's main island.

Almost every Japanese citizen, including myself, experienced the horror of daily carpet bombing by several hundred B-12 bombers for many months in 1944–1945 and witnessed the devastation of many cities in Japan. Many Japanese felt that they were used inhumanely as guinea pigs after the experience of such a horrendous holocaust in their motherland.

This event obviously marked a new

Atomic Age of mankind, resulting in the
rethinking of ethical philosophy in the new world
order. Nevertheless, twenty-three years elapsed
before the major powers attempted to curtail
further development of this horrendous bomb by
signing the Treaty on the Non-Proliferation of
Nuclear Weapons in July 1968. Unfortunately, this
treaty turned out to be a small success because
the world superpowers conducted nuclear tests
during the Cold War era and manufactured and
stored a large number of atomic bombs sufficient
to kill the entire population of the world several
hundred times over. Even after the Berlin Wall
was torn down, nuclear tests were still periodically
conducted.

Many American and Europeans have also
decried the immoral use of weapons such as the
atomic bomb which exceeded the killing power of
poison gases and biological weapons. After the
atomic bombings, not only the *hibakusha* in
Hiroshima and Nagasaki but many Japanese
wondered why the United Nations and the major
powers did not ban atomic bombs as they did
chemical and biological weapons.

After the bombing, the people of Hiroshima and Nagasaki were physically and mentally shattered, enduring considerable fear in expressing their anger and agony over the nature and magnitude of atomic weapons. When the U.S. Armed Forces occupied the country, the Japanese fear of American reprisal became more intense and made them conceal their emotions against the atomic bomb. Hence, they refused to publicize their horrible experiences for many years, although some quietly expressed their sadness and sorrow in poems and articles.

In September 1945, almost all of the Japanese publications related to the atomic bomb casualties were censored and suppressed by the authority of the Special Press Code issued by the Allied Forces GHQ Information Service. This decree lasted for six years and eight months and the banned manuscripts, books and photographs were secretly sent to a United States Government agency. Only recently have these materials been released from the Library of Congress and other U.S. library archives by the Freedom of Information Act.

Thousands of the mentally and physically disfigured *hibakusha* have lived miserable lives and gradually died of complications from the atomic bombing without financial aid from either the Japanese government or any charitable organizations. Some committed suicide due to severe mental depression. In the past twenty years, however, the surviving family members and their friends have begun to express their experiences in poetry, novels and paintings.

For the past twelve centuries, the Japanese people have expressed their intense pent-up emotions in tanka, one of the most unique and shortest forms of poetic expression in the world. Most samurai wrote *jisei* (deathbed tanka) at the site of their hara-kiri. It was natural for many *hibakusha* to write tanka during the time of their suffering prior to death. Several years after the end of World War II, the literary editor of a newspaper in Hiroshima invited its readers, many *hibakusha* and their relatives, to submit tanka concerning their experiences about the bombing. The responses were overwhelming; more than 6,500 tanka poems were submitted. One of the master tanka poets and *hibakusha*, Seishi Toyota,

and his friends painstakingly selected approxi-
mately 1,000 poems published in the tanka
anthology, *Kashū Hiroshima*.

Toyota noted that the best tanka poems
on the atomic bomb were not written by the
famous master poets but rather by the *hibakusha*
themselves, the amateur poets. It seems that
well-known poets sought to depict the immeasur-
ably destructive energy of the atomic bomb by
hyperbole. By contrast, the *hibakusha* wrote their
tanka using simple words and achieved success.

Toyota and other scholars have published
several commentaries and tanka anthologies on
the atomic bomb. However, these publications
were not widely circulated outside of Japan and
had little impact on the West. A great number of
tanka poets intended to express their agony and
pain to a wide audience in an effort to terminate
the manufacture and use of the atomic bomb on
this earth.

This anthology was compiled by selecting
the best 100 tanka poems of 100 poets from
several anthologies published up to 1993. Almost
all the poets are atomic bomb casualties and

approximately sixty percent of them died shortly after or within ten years of the war. (Poets who are deceased are denoted by a mark, +, next to their name in the text.)

Each tanka was written in 5 lines (5-7-5-7-7 jion) and this collection includes the kanji and the Hepburn style roma-ji. Most tanka masters classified tanka poems into two types, masurao-uta (masculine tanka) and taoyame-uta (feminine tanka). In masurao-uta, the poets used kanji (Chinese characters) as well as poetic phrases taken from 5th century Chinese literature and poems. In taoyame-uta, poets used yamato-kotoba (aboriginal Japanese words) with hirakana (the Japanese alphabet). Many tanka poets still use some archaic hirakana in their poems. In this anthology we have tried to respect the poets' original form as much as possible and have used the archaic hirakana when it was used in the original tanka. Some readers will notice some variations in the hirakana in this anthology.

As a youth in Japan, I witnessed the miserable death of many hibakusha soldiers and civilians who returned from Hiroshima to their native villages. Like a bad dream, I still remember a soldier whose face was pale as a ghost, suffering from bloody diarrhea before his death. People in the world have been bombarded with statistical data concerning the atomic bombing but have never heard of the outcry of the *hibakusha*. Will this anthology become a collection of the *jisei* of the *hibakusha* to plead for the abolition of atomic weapons and peace on earth? Reading and translating these tanka, I could not help but feel humble in the wake of the suffering of the dead and presently ailing *hibakusha* in Hiroshima and Nagasaki. I feel that this anthology will be a requiem to all *hibakusha* and pray for peace and enlightenment of their souls. They are the tragic victims of this abominable weapon.

Jiro Nakano

TAKAKO ASHIDA+

芦田高子

A crying girl

whose face is covered

with keloids,

we can only wipe the tears

off our own faces.

ケロイドの

顔を曝らして

泣くひとを

支えむ涙

誰も誰も拭く

keroido no

kao wo sarashite

naku hito wo

sasaen namida

tare mo tare mo fuku

AYAKO ETSUCHI+

越智　紋子

Like a demon or ghost,

a man runs away—

staggering—

with both hands

hung loosely in front of him.

もろ手みな

前に垂して

よろめきつ

幽鬼にも似し

人が逃げ行く

morote mina

mae ni tarashite

yoromekitsu

yūki nimo nishi

hito ga nigeyuku

ITSUMA FUJII

藤井逸馬

Your souls

that have fallen

in the turbid waters,

may they rest

in the river of man.

濁りたる

流れに落ちし

魂魄の

浮かぶ瀬あれよ

にんげんの河

nigoritaru

nagareni ochishi

konpaku no

ukabu se areyo

ningen no kawa

FUMIKO FUJII+

藤井文子

Tonight again,

the only light to aid me

as I write my nursing notes—

the luminous flames

from the burning of the corpses.

人を焼く

焔の明りを

たよりとし

こよひも看護の

メモをしたたむ

hito wo yaku

honoho no akari wo

tayori to shi

koyoi mo kango no

memo wo shitatamu

ICHIO FUKUSHIMA+

死ぬということ

Keloids!

Unbearably grotesque

on human faces.

Walk into the crowds

and display them!

ケロイドは

人類の醜い

貌だ

雑踏の中に

さらして歩け

keroido wa

jinrui no minikui

kao da

zattō no naka ni

sarashite aruke

YOSHIHIKO FURUYOSHI

古吉義彦

To die for your country

has been demeaned.

Look at the soldiers

lying dead,

without shoes!

国のため

死ぬということ

見下ろされ

転がりている

裸足の兵ら

kuni no tame

shinu to yūkoto

miorosare

korogarite iru

rasoku no heira

KIYO HAKUSHIMA+

白島きよ

Once again

summer has come.

Beneath the grass,

lay hidden ten thousand

angered souls.

ここにまた

夏は来たりて

草茂る

地に幾万の

怒りはひそむ

koko ni mata

natsu wa kitarite

kusa shigeru

chi ni ikuman no

ikari wa hisomu

YŌKO HAMADA+

浜田陽子

You raised that same hand

which made the genocide.

Are you blind to the blood

of the holocaust

that circulates through your hand!

大量殺戮

かく人間の

手がなすを

その手をかざせ

血が透きて見ゆ

jenosaido

kaku ningen no

te ga nasu wo

sono te wo kazase

chi ga tokite miyu

SEISAKU HASEGAWA+

長谷川精作

Alas—

in the midst of sandbanks,

the red glow of burning bodies

done by us,

the survivors.

川中の

州にあかあかと

人焼けり

あわれ人焼けり

生きのこりゐて

kawanaka no

su ni akaaka to

hito yakeri

aware hito yakeri

iki nokori ite

SHIZUE HATSUI+

初井しづ枝

A photo of a school boy—

his face agonized with pain—

fingers stripped of nails.

Is there a message

to be heard?

苦しさに

もがきて剥ぎし

生爪ありて

写真の学童が

語るならずや

kurushisa ni

mogakite hagishi

tsume arite

shashin no gakudō ga

kataru narazuya

YUZURU HAYASE+

早瀬　譲

Radiation concealed

in a muscle—

science reveals

merely its science,

a giant flame.

肉片に

ひそむ放射能の

きびしさを

科学は見しむ

炎のさまに

nikuhen ni

hisomu hōshanō

kibishisa wo

kagaku wa mishimu

honoho no sama ni

OSAMU HIKINO+

引野 収

Anti-nuclear movement

lies in "Denial of Death."

True words

are simple,

direct.

反核は

「死の拒否」にあり

真実の

ことば単純にして

直接なり

hankaku wa

shi no kyohi ni ari

shinjitsu no

kotoba tanjun ni shite

chokusetsu nari

KATSUKO HISAOKA

久岡勝子

College students obediently

saluted to the command,

"Die for the country!"

All are killed

in the war.

死ねよとの

命令にさえ

挙手の礼

返して逝きし

学徒還らず

shine yo to no

meirei ni sae

kyoshu no rei

kaeshite yukishi

gakuto kaerazu

SHŌZŌ HORI+

堀　正三

"We will never repeat

this error again,"

appears in an apology.

A disgrace to any nation

that used this adage.

「過ちは

繰り返しませぬ

から」と書く

かかる卑屈に

なれし民族

"ayamachi wa

kurikaeshi masenu

kara" to kaku

kakaru hikutsu ni

nareshi minzoku

SEISHŪ HOZUMI

穂積生秋

The Americans

have licked the core

of your inner organ!

Drip with sweat.

Defend yourself. Please!

アメリカに

臓腑の裏も

舐められて

汗じっとりと

個を守らんとする

amerika ni

zōfu no ura mo

namerarete

ase jittori to

ko wo mamoranto suru

SEITAI I

尹　政泰

Where is the agony
of the Hiroshima massacre?
The doves are flying away,
leaving the charred
Koreans alone.

ひろしまの
誅はいずこ
灼かれたる
鮮人措きて
翔けりゆく鳩

hiroshima no

itami wa izuko

yakaretaru

senjin okite

kakeri yuku hato

SHIZUKO IGUCHI+

井口静子

Thirty years have gone;

but his ghost will never

vanish from memory.

My husband killed by the bomb

still saddens my soul.

三十年

今にして去らぬ

わが脳裡に

爆死せし夫

目裏にさびし

sanjūnen

ima nishite saranu

waga nōri ni

bakushi seshi tsuma

maura ni sabishi

MOMOYO ISHII+

石井百代

Mothers, wives, sisters
and grandmothers—
remember your losses.
Stand up and fill those prisons.
Defy the draft!

徴兵は
命かけても
阻むべし
母、祖母、おみな
牢に満つるとも

chōhei wa

inochi kakete mo

kobamu beshi

haha, sobo, omina

rō ni mitsurutomo

NOBUKO ISHIKAWA

石川乃婦子

The exterior

of the Hiroshima Dome

is painted snow white.

Is it an effort to whitewash

Hiroshima's pain?

粧おあれし

ドームの肌の

白々と

とり澄ましたる

影は痛まず

yosoowareshi

dōmu no hada no

shirajira to

torisumashitaru

kage wa itamazu

SADAKO ISHII+

石井貞子

One that lies down

is not a corpse—

he is still breathing,

wriggling—

here lies a living being.

まろべるは

屍ならず

呼吸ありて

かそかにうごめく

命ころがる

maroberu wa

shikabane narazu

iki arite

kasokani ugomeku

inochi korogaru

TERUKO ISHIBASHI+

石橋照子

I sit down to halt

the Atomic Bomb testing.

The clogs I take off

cast clear-cut

shadows.

原子爆弾

実験阻止と

坐り込む

吾がぬぎし下駄の

刻明な影

genshi bakudan

jikken soshi to

suwarikomu

waga nugishi geta no

kokumei na kage.

MASANORI ICHIOKA+

市岡正憲

Another anti-nuclear petition?

A mother who lost her two sons

in the war

refuses to sign

again.

吾が子ふたり

戦に亡くせし

母なるに

核廃絶の

署名を拒む

waga ko futari

ikusa ni nakuseshi

haha naruni

kaku haizetsu no

shomei wo kobamu

TOKUZABURŌ IMAI+

今井篤三郎

The streets
still smoldering,
are deserted.
"Let me hear a voice
calling your father!"

余燼くゆる
巷もとほり
うつつなし
父よばふ声
そこにあらぬか

yojin kuyuru

chimata mo tōri

utsutsu nashi

chichi yobau koe

soko ni aranuka

HARUE IMAMOTO+

今元　春江

"Run under the beam!"

my dying wife cried out to me.

I will never marry

because of what I saw

in her eyes.

梁の下

逃げよと言いし

亡き妻よ

その瞳ゆえ

未だめとらず

hari no shita

nigeyo to iishi

naki tsuma yo

sono hitomi yue

imada metorazu

SEIKAN INOUE+

井上清幹

Half scorched pieces

of brains and throats

lie next to each other

on the bottom floor

of a burnt air-raid shelter.

焼け穴の

びちやつく底に

ころげいる

生やけのままの

脳髄とのど

yakeana no

bichatsuku soko ni

koroge iru

namayake no mama no

nōzui to nodo

YUKIE ITAMASU+

板舛雪江

Lonely rainy night—

the phosphorous fires

glow in eerie colors

like hatred seen

in human eyes.

粛条と

夜の雨ふれば

焼跡のそこかしこ

憎しみの眼の

色の如くもゆる

shōjō to

yo no ame fureba

yakeato no sokokashiko

nikushimi no me no

iro no gotoku moyuru

HIROSHI IWAMOTO+

岩本　浩

The deployment of

"Tomahawk" missiles can begin

a nuclear crisis.

Refusing the leaflet

will not let you escape untouched.

トマホーク

配備がひらく

核の危機

ビラ受け取らぬ

ものも逃れず

tomahōku

haibi ga hiraku

kaku no kiki

bira uketoranu

mono mo nogarezu

ASAO IZUMI

泉　朝雄

On newspapers

spread on depot platforms,

we sleep

with those

already dead.

新聞紙の束

ひろげてホームに

眠る中

すでに屍と

なりしも交じる

shinbunshi no taba

hirogete hōmu ni

nemuru naka

sude ni kabane to

narishi mo majiru

TOSHIE JŌDEN

城田斗志恵

The Atomic Bomb

destroyed Hiroshima,

but her rivers

still flow

glitteringly.

原爆に

すべて焼かれし

ヒロシマの

川は死なざりき

煌き流る

genbaku ni

subete yakareshi

hiroshima no

kawa wa shinazariki

kirameki nagaru

TSUGIO KAGAWA

加川次男

This morning upon awakening
I heard the loud cicadas.
My thoughts return
to that summer
when it was *Ashura*.*

目覚むれば
すでに時雨るる
蝉の声
いのち一夏
修羅となりたる

mezamureba

sude ni shigururu

semi no koe

inochi hitonatsu

shura to naritaru

(*a hell or inferno)

MIKIO KANDA

神田三亀男

Overflowing

the orbita,

maggots crawl on

the senseless face;

they are stronger than man.

眼窩より

溢れし蛆は

知覚なき

顔面を這えり

人より強く

ganka yori

afureshi uji wa

chikaku naki

ganmen wo haeri

hito yori tsuyoku

SADAO KATAOKA+

片岡貞雄

Suddenly

the street is darkened.

Black evening shower

is falling profusely

on the corpses.

たちまちに

街は翳りて

のべつなき

死体をたたく

黒き夕立

tachimachi ni

machi wa kagerite

nobetsu naki

shitai wo tataku

kuroki yūdachi

TERUKO KATŌ+

加藤輝子

Blades of young grass

grow vigorously

through the cracks

of the severely

damaged *Genbaku* Dome.*

原爆ドームの

くずれ落ちたる

すき間から

生生しく育つ

若草の一もと

genbaku dōmu no

kuzure ochitaru

sukima kara

namanamashiku sodatsu

wakakusa no hitomoto

(*The *Genbaku* Dome, or atomic bomb dome, refers to the shell of
one of the few remaining buildings left standing in Hiroshima after
the bombing.)

OSAMU KIMATA+

木俣　修

Let the voice of a girl

blind with keloids,

resound

over that country

beyond the ocean!

ケロイドに

かの日盲し

をとめのこえ

海越えてかの

国にひびけよ

keroido ni

kano hi meshiishi

otome no koe

umi koete kano

kuni ni hibikeyo

FUSAKO KIMURA

木村房子

As clothes

left from the burning fires

wave in the air,

the wailing voices of the *hibakusha*

shall enwrap the world.

灼け残りし

檻衣翳して

訴うる

ヒバクシャの声

世界をつつめ

yake nokorishi

ran'i kazashite

uttauru

hibakusha no koe

sekai wo tsutsume

ITARU KŌCHI+

河内　格

The rain is falling

on the white bones

of those who died

at the epicenter,

along with tiles and pebbles.

爆心地に

死したる人の

白き骨

瓦礫と共に

雨に打たるる

bakushinchi ni

shishitaru hito no

shiroki hone

gareki to tomo ni

ame ni utaruru

HIROSHI KŌMOTO+

河本　弘

I walk

aimlessly.

in darkness,

the lit Dome floats

like a wax grave.

たどきなく

歩む彼方の

闇に浮き

屍蝋のごとし

灯るドームは

tadoki naku

ayumu kanata no

yami ni uki

shirō no gotoshi

tomoru dōmu wa

YOSHIKO KŌMOTO

河本芳子

I know, as a man

with good grace,

I should be gone by now;

yet, I keep working

using my sick leave.

いさぎよく

人間なれば

去るべきを

知りつつ病欠

がちに勤むる

isagiyoku

ningen nareba

sarubeki wo

shiritsutsu byōketsu

gachi ni tsutomuru

YOSHIMI KONDŌ

近藤芳美

The white mushroom cloud

has risen

in the white empty sky—

its ghost lingers

in the city of death.

白き虚空

とどまり白き

原子雲

そのまぼろしに

つづく死の町

shiroki kokū

todomari shiroki

genshigumo

sono maboroshi ni

tsuzuku shi no machi

YOSHIKO KŌNO+

河野淑子

Not knowing

his mother is dead,

a blind infant

looks for

her breast.

こと切れし

母とも知らず

その乳を

まさぐるよこの

盲ひたる児は

kotokireshi

haha tomo shirazu

sono chichi wo

masaguruyo kono

meshiitaru ko wa

AYAO KOYAMA+

小山綾夫

Into the desolate scene

of burnt shops and buildings

in Hiroshima,

several shadows

walk aimlessly.

燃ゆるもの

燃え尽くしたる

広島を

消然とゆく

人影いくつ

moyuru mono

moetsukushi taru

hiroshima wo

shōzen to yuku

hitokage ikutsu

YOSHIMITSU KOZAKAI+

小堺吉光

Late at night,

in the corner

of the bombed ruins,

water glitters

like a living creature.

焼跡の

更けゆく夜の

一隅に

生きもののごと

水光るなり

yakeato no

fukeyuku yoru no

ichigū ni

ikimono no goto

mizu hikaru nari

MISAKO MASUDA+

益田美佐子

I look at

each boy's corpse.

"Is it my son?"

I draw my face close,

then I leave.

少年の

屍を見れば

顔よせて

吾子ならじかと

覗きては行く

shōnen no

kabane wo mireba

kao yosete

ako narajika to

nozokite wa yuku

REISUKE MASUDA+

益田礼助

Without a word,

my wife returns.

She offers a small urn

from her arms

and begins to weep.

帰り来し

妻は答へず

泣き伏して

抱ける小箱を

われに差出す

kaeri kishi

tsuma wa kotaezu

naki fushite

idakeru kobako wo

ware ni sashidasu

CHIYOJI MATSUMOTO

松本千代二

The road to a nuclear free world

shines brightly

in a straight line.

My dream to see its end

is way yonder.

ひとすじの

反核の道

かがやけり

わが夢にして

はるかなる道

hitosuji no

hankaku no michi

kagayakeri

waga yume ni shite

harukanaru michi

SHŌFŪ MATSUMURA+
松村松風

It is a living mess

for this old survivor,

standing in line

to register my name

in the attendance book.

汗拭きつつ

出勤簿捺す

列にあり

生き残る身の

老いの生きざま

ase fukitsutsu

shukkinbō osu

retsu ni ari

iki nokoru mi no

oi no ikizama

REIKO MIKUNI+

三国玲子

If you so wish,

cry for the National Defense,

but first

stand and round up

your own son!

国防を

言うならば言へ

先ず起ちて

その子を狩れよ

みずからの子を

kokubō

yūnaraba ie

mazu tachite

sono ko wo kareyo

mizukara no ko wo

KAICHI MITA

三田嘉一

Are they still reflected

in your misty eyes?

The thirsty children

who drowned sliding down

into this river.

濡るる瞳に

映れるものか

水欲ると

河になだれて

果てし子らはも

nururu me ni

utsureru mono ka

mizu horu to

kawa ni nadarete

hateshi kora wamo

KEN'ICHI MIYAGI+

宮城謙一

I will overcome

the shattering of my mind

by the atomic bomb.

I shall decide the redirection

of my remaining life.

原爆の

慄身のうちを

貫きて

わが残る生の

行方決しぬ

genbaku no

risshin no uchi wo

tsuranukite

waga nokoru sei no

yukue kesshinu

SADAMU MIYATA

宮田　定

I see the procession

of burnt sores

on disfigured faces

and pray for my younger brother

to be dead by now.

焼けただれ

顔形なき

列つづき

弟よ死んで

をれよとも思ふ

yake tadare

kao katachi naki

retsu tsuzuki

otōto yo shinde

oreyo tomo omou

HATSUKO MIYAMAE

宮前初子

A crowd of ten thousand

are standing in despair

with skins hanging

from red sores—

the scorched land of Hiroshima.

赤むけの

皮膚垂れし群れ

幾万が

広島の土

わが踏みて立つ

akamuke no

hifu tareshi mure

ikuman ga

hiroshima no tsuchi

waga fumite tatsu

MASAYOSHI MIYAMOTO+

宮本まさよし

A few survivors

are looking at a rainbow

that appeared

over the horizon

of the endless burnt land.

かぎりなく

つづく焦土の

果に立つ

虹見る幾人か

いま生きてゐて

kagiri naku

tsuzuku shōdo no

hate ni tatsu

niji miru ikutari ka

ima ikite ite

SHIZUKA MIYAMOTO+

宮本静香

Exhausted, I sew.

My tired body

is filled with thin blood.

My distorted vision begins

to shape that summer cloud.

うすき血を

秘めてけだるく

もの縫う日

歪むわが瞳に

夏雲を追う

usuki chi wo

himete kedaruku

mono nuu hi

hizumu waga me ni

natsugumo wo ou

HIROSHI MORISHITA

森下　弘

A *kappa** is walking

in front of my eyes

a burnt head

distinctly losing

its shape in my cap.

くっきりと

帽子の痕残し

火傷せる

河童が我の

目の前歩む

kukkiri to

bōshi no ato nokoshi

yakedo seru

kappa ga ware no

me no mae ayumu

(*river spirit or imp)

HIROKO NAGAI

永井弘子

Millions of sons drafted

by the Emperor are dead—

the voices of the mothers,

calling their names,

fill the moors and hills of Japan.

天皇に

召され死にし子を

呼ぶ母の

声日本の

山野に充つる

tennō ni

mesare shinishi ko wo

yobu haha no

koe nippon no

sanya ni mitsuru

TAKASHI NAGAI+

永井　隆

In the middle of the flame
at the burnt offering rite,
a girl with white lilies,
alas, begins to be burnt
as she keeps singing!

燔祭の
ほのほの中に
うたひつつ
白百合乙女は
燃えにけるかも

hansai no
honoho no naka ni
utai tsutsu
shirayuri otome wa
moe ni kerukamo

KIYOTO NAKAMURA+

中邑浄人

At the riverside,

in a position

to drink water,

this soldier is

already dead.

川べりに

伏して水飲む

姿勢せる

この兵もすでに

死してゐるなり

kawaberi ni

fushite mizu nomu

shisei seru

kono hei mo sudeni

shishite irunari

MASAYO NAKAMOTO

仲本政代

Ten thousands or more

sank into this river—

today still flowing

soundlessly,

its surface motionless.

幾万の

いのち沈めし

川の面の

動かざるごと

今日も流れゆく

ikuman no

inochi shizumeshi

kawa no mo no

ugokazaru goto

kyō mo nagare yuku

AIKO NAKAZAWA+

中沢愛子

Together with my sister,

I am leaving Hiroshima,

carrying the urn

of my mother's ashes

on my back.

白骨と

なりたる母を

背に負いて

妹と二人

ひろしまを去る

hakkotsu to

naritaru haha wo

se ni oite

imōto to futari

hiroshima wo saru

CHIHIRO NISHIMOTO

西元千展

Like rotted wood,

a corpse is obstructed

at the bridge girder,

then it flows away

without being seen by anyone.

朽木のごとく

死体は橋桁に

つとかかり

顧る人もなければ

流れゆきたり

kuchiki no gotoku

shitai wa hashigeta ni

tsuto kakari

miru hito mo nakereba

nagare yuki tari

KIMIKO NISHIOKA

西岡喜美子

Human beings

with gorged eyeballs

and melted cells

have become photo objects.

Hiroshima summer!

眼は抉られ

細胞溶けし

人間が

被写体にさる

ヒロシマの夏

me wa egurare

saibō tokeshi

ningen ga

hishatai ni saru

hiroshima no natsu

TOSHIE NISHIOKU+

西奥とし江

Side-stepping the many corpses

of the *hibakusha*, I run away—

the devil's heart

must lie concealed

inside of me.

原爆の

死者をまたぎて

逃げたりし

鬼の心を

われはひそめもつ

genbaku no

shisha wo matagite

nigetarishi

oni no kokoro wo

ware wa hisome motsu

MIDORI NITTA+

新田みどり

Each time I walk

the valley road

to return to my native land,

I carry the remains

of my husband and child.

ふるさとの

峡の細道

夫と子の

遺骨抱きて

通ふ幾度び

furusato no

kai no hosomichi

tsuma to ko no

ikotsu idakite

kayou ikutabi

TAKAYOSHI NITTA

新田隆義

The statue stands

covered with shining dewdrops

Peace will not come

with one person's prayer

alone.

全身に

露ひかりつつ

像は立つ

祈るのみにては

平和は近づかぬ

zenshin ni

tsuyu hikari tsutsu

zō wa tatsu

inoru nomi nitewa

heiwa wa chikazukanu

HISATO NOGAMI

野上久人

Crape myrtle—

falls secretly

to turn into a flame;

poignant stillness in Japan

during a period of mourning.

さるすべり

花ひそひそと

散りて炎ゆ

日本の忌の

鋭き静寂

sarusuberi

hana hisohiso to

chirite moyu

nippon no ki no

surudoki shijima

HAYATARŌ NUMANAKA+

沼中早太郎

Under the summer sun,

I caress the monument

of the Atomic Bomb

and listen to the voices

rising from within.

夏陽射す

原爆の碑に

掌は触れて

起る声なき

もの聴かむとす

natsuhi sasu

genbaku no hi ni

te wa furete

okoru koe naki

mono kikan tosu

TADAO ŌGIHATA

扇畑忠雄

Severely charred

by the Atomic Bomb,

the eucalyptus trees

of our native land

have become today's ghosts!

原爆に

焼けただれたる

ふるさとの

ユーカリ樹わが

今日のまぼろし

genbaku ni

yake tadare taru

furusato no

yūkariju waga

kyō no maboroshi

HISAKO ŌSUGI

大杉久子

At broad daylight,

a peony flower is

exposing its pistil—

life, as whenever asked,

passes away!

真昼間に

花芯さらせる

牡丹あり

いつにても問う

命よぎるを

mahiruma ni

kashin saraseru

botan ari

itsu nitemo tou

inochi yogiru wo

SHIZUKO ŌTA+

太田静子

The constant search

for a loved one

in the city of Hiroshima

seems eternal—

looking for life among the dead.

探しつつ

出合うとみえて

また逸れつ

広島は死にし

者を追う街

sagashi tsutsu

deau to miete

mata nogaretsu

hiroshima wa shinishi

mono wo ou machi

TOMOO ŌZAWA+

大沢張夫

Burnt and ulcerated,

a blind infant

searches furtively,

calling and calling

his mother's name.

焼けただれ

盲となりし

幼子が

母の名呼びて

さ迷ひをれり

yake tadare

meshihi to narishi

osanago ga

haha no na yobite

samayoi oreri

CHIE SETOGUCHI+

瀬戸口千枝

I still hear their voices

crying in agony—

scorched bodies

clinging to the iron wires

of the burnt prison.

鉄窓に

すがりつ焼かれし

人の声

刑務所跡に

立ちて聞きゐつ

tessō ni

sugaritsu yakareshi

hito no koe

keimusho ato ni

tachite kiki itsu

AKIRA SHIMA+

島　昭

Gone is everyone

who I have relied upon.

I am now bathing

under the midday sun

with memories of what was.

憑めりし

人の尽一

ほろびたり

かく思い陽を

頭に浴びゐたり

tanomerishi

hito no kotogoto

horobi tari

kaku omoi hi wo

zu ni abi itari

HACHIRŌ SHIMAUCHI+

島内八郎

Facing a garden stone

that never glistens

even by sprinkling water,

I realize the Atomic Bomb

has killed even the stone.

打水にも

光沢顕たぬ

庭石に

対ひをり原爆は

石も殺しぬ

uchimizu nimo

kōtaku tatanu

niwaishi ni

aiori genbaku wa

ishi mo koroshinu

SHINOE SHŌDA+
正田篠枝

The large skull

is the teacher's.

Gathered

around it,

smaller skulls.

大き骨は

先生ならむ

そのそばに

小さき頭の

骨あつまれり

ooki na hone wa

sensei naran

sono soba ni

chiisaki atama no

hone atsumareri

FUMIKO SHŌJI

小路文子

A man's life is imprinted vividly

on the step stone.

The crime cannot be eradicated

despite the fading

of its "death shadow."

人の生命

石のきざわし

烙きつけり

科消されまじ

「死の影」薄るとも

hito no inochi

ishi no kizawashi

yaki tsukeri

toga kesaremaji

shi no kage usuru tomo

SUMIKO SHINPU

信夫澄子

Sleeping each night

alongside the neighboring

nuclear weapons,

how can we escape

readily from our own death?

核兵器と

となりあわせの

夜の眠り

やすやすと死に

救われるものか

kakuheiki to

tonari awase no

yo no nemuri

yasuyasu to shi ni

sukuwareru mono ka

YUTAKA SHIRAKI+

白木　裕

At high tide

in this burnt city,

neither parents nor children

will come to see the corpses

floating in the river.

焼けし街の

川に潮差し

浮き漂ふ

この骸らに

親も子も来ず

yakeshi machi no

kawa ni shio sashi

uki tadayou

kono mukurora ni

oya mo ko mo kozu

SHIGEO SUGINO

杉野繁男

After robbing us

of our sons and daughters,

they order us to win the war.

No one has known

the road to peace.

息子を奪い

娘を奪いて

勝てという

平和の底の

知られざる道

musuko wo ubai

musume wo ubaite

kate to iu

heiwa no soko no

chirare zaru michi

HATSUYO SUGITA+

杉田はつよ

Today I shall

burn a little girl

in a potato patch

where I burned

her brother yesterday.

五歳の子

焼いた小さな

諸畑の

くぼみで今日は

その妹を焼く

gosai no ko

yaita chiisana

imohata no

kubomi de kyō wa

sono imōto wo yaku

TSUTOMI SUZUKI+

鈴木つとみ

Politicians

who deceive people

do not commit suicide;

they are only gasping

for a nuclear war.

国民を

だまし続ける

為政者ら

自決もなさず

核に喘げり

kokumin wo

damashi tsuzukeru

iseishara

jiketsu mo nasazu

kaku ni aegeri

TAKEO TAKAHASHI+

高橋武夫

You should be satisfied

if every living being

perished to become

a dead man

in this world!

天地の

死塊となりて

生きものの

みな滅びなば

慰むものを

ametsuchi no

shikai to narite

ikimono no

mina horobi naba

nagusamu mono wo

KANAE TAKANO

高野　鼎

I have lost six children

to the Atomic Bomb.

In my sorrow, I stand to walk

but wish to scream

at the top of my voice.

吾子六人

原爆に奪はれし

悲しみに

立ちて歩めど

わめき立てたく

ako rokunin

genbaku ni ubawareshi

kanashimi ni

tachite ayumedo

wameki tatetaku

KUNIYO TAKAYASU+

高安国世

He no longer lives,

that man who once sang

of a flower

blooming

on earth.

天地の

崩るる下の

一輪の

花をうたいし

人もまた亡し

ametsuchi no

kuzururu shita no

ichirin no

hana wo utaishi

hito mo mata nashi

ICHISAKU TAKEUCHI+

竹内一作

Although I live,
I am given a funeral service
on August 6:
my anniversary day
of dying.

生きながら
吾は祭られ
ありしなり
八月六日を
命日として

iki nagara

ware wa matsurare

arishi nari

hachi gatsu muika wo

meinichi to shite

HIROSHI TAKEYAMA

竹山　広

The corpses of those

who once met here

now fill this Eternal River

as water rises

at dark tide.

くろぐろと

水満ち水に

うち合へる死者

満ちてわが

とこしなへの川

kuroguro to

mizu michi mizu ni

uchi aeru shisha

michite waga

tokoshinae no kawa

KURAMOTO TANIGUCHI+

谷口蔵素

Evening clouds

dyed the color of blood

glow over the river

where ten thousand and more

are submerged.

茜雲

血の色なして

幾万の

生命沈めし

川の面に映ゆ

akane gumo

chi no iro nashite

ikuman no

seimei shizumeshi

kawa no mo ni hayu

KAZUE TASAKA

田阪数江

Undestroyed

but beautified,

the *Genbaku* Dome

is forever casting

a heartless shadow.

美化されし

原爆ドーム

崩壊の

術なく非情の

澄む影を見す

bika sareshi

genbaku dōmu

hōkai no

sube naku hijō no

sumu kage wo mizu

NOBUE TASHIMA

田島伸枝

The corpses of those

who died of persecution

caused by the *genbaku;**

was each death

mere dirt?

死はいづれも

泥土のごとしか

迫害に

果てしししむら

原爆下の民

shi wa izuremo

deido no gotoshi ka

hakugai ni

hateshi shishimura

genbakuka no tami

(*atomic bomb)

EI TAYA

田谷　鋭

Two score and more lines

drawn to study

the epicenter

cross sharply

on a sheet of graph paper.

爆心地を

究むと引きし

幾十の

線の交差鋭し

図表のうへに

bakushinchi wo

kiwamu to hikishi

ikujū no

sen no kōsa toshi

zuhyō no ue ni

KUNIO TOYOHARA

豊原国夫

Wild birds silently
eat the decayed flesh.
The luminous flames
continue to consume
the dead bodies.

腐肉食む
野鳥声なく
炎々と
屍こがし
勃火燃えつぐ

funiku hamu

yachō koe naku

en'en to

shikabane kogashi

bokka moe tsugu

豊田清史

A *hibaku* woman,

who refused my help

to the bathroom last night,

is found dead cold

on the dirt floor this morning.

取るわがて

拒みて尿に

ゆきし女

暁寒く

土間に絶え居る

toru waga te

kobamite nyō ni

yukishi hito

akatsuki samuku

doma ni tae iru

KOICHIRO TOZAWA

杜沢光一郎

Cicadas continuously sing,

until their mouths ache

to protest

the two memorial days

of the Atomic Bombing.

原爆忌

ふたつもつこと

椒の

口疼くがに

蝉鳴きしきる

genbakuki

futatsu motsu koto

hajikami no

kuchi hibiku gani

semi naki shikiru

MASANA TSUMURA+

津村正名

"The voices of Neptune"*

gradually die

into a distance,

their bloody lives

shall never return.

いつの日か

「わだつみの声」

遠のきぬ

血の還らざる

生命ふたたび

itsuno hi ka

wadatsumi no koe

tō nokinu

chi no kaerazaru

inochi futatabi

(* Diaries of the college students who died during World War II)

EIZŌ UCHIDA+

内田英三

Her burnt face swollen,

a naked girl

grabs my foot,

begs for water

as she falls on the ground.

火ぶくれに

なりて裸に

倒れゐる

処女水欲る

吾が足つかみて

hibukure ni

narite hadaka ni

taore iru

otome mizu horu

waga ashi tsukamite

YOSHIKO UCHIKOSHI

打越嘉子

He led the free life,

never doubting the war cause.

Now his long legs

are twisted, bent,

to fit into his coffin.

奔放に

生きてうたがい

持たざりし

柩にあまる

足折り曲げる

honpō ni

ikite utagai

motazarishi

hitsugi ni amaru

ashi ori mageru

KIYOKO UCHIMI

内海清子

In this river,

the silent voices

of ten thousand and more

are lingering

like a subdued curse.

この川に

ただよい果てし

幾万の

呪阻とも声なき

声に佇む

kono kawa ni

tadayoi hateshi

ikuman no

juso tomo koe naki

koe ni tatazumu

有良佳寿

If you are armed,

stop your foolishness.

Shout against the nuclear weapons—

declare your neutrality

after disarming yourself!

武装して

反核叫ぶ

愚をやめよ

武装を解きて

中立宣言

busō shite

hankaku sakebu

gū wo yameyo

busō wo tokite

chūritsusengen

TOMIKO YAMAGUCHI

山口富美子

Her screams

have ceased today—

the death of a woman

who lost her hair and mind

is reported.

叫び声

今日とだえゐき

髪ぬけて

狂ひし女の

死を伝へ来る

sakebi koe

kyō todae iki

kami nukete

kuruishi hito no

shi wo tsutae kuru

HAKUTEI YASUDA+

保田白汀

After the screaming,

the scars, the scorched land,

I see the unhealed city,

when I hear the sound

of pebbles as I till my land.

叫喚の

痕の起伏も

癒えざるに

寸土を掘れば

瓦礫の音す

kyōkan no

ato no kifuku mo

iezaru ni

sundo wo horeba

gareki no oto su

KAORU YASUI+

安井　郁

The Atomic Bomb

killed indiscriminately—

anyone—

even American prisoners of war

incarcerated in Hiroshima.

原爆は

何の差別も

なさざりき

広島に死す

米兵捕虜も

genbaku wa

nan no sabetsu mo

nasazariki

hiroshima ni shisu

beihei horyo mo

REFERENCES

Maruki, Toshi. *Hiroshima no Pika [Atomic Bomb and Hiroshima]*. Tokyo: Komine Shoten, 1980.

Nakano, Jiro. "Yoshiko Matsuda, a Tanka Poetess of Hawaii." *Kaimana* Winter/Spring 1991: 19–30.

Nakano, Jiro. "Honolulu Tanka Club: The Choon-shisha." *Hawaii Herald*, July 16, 1993: A12–A13.

Nakano, Jiro and Kay Nakano, eds. *Poets Behind Barbed Wire*. Honolulu, Hawaii: Bamboo Ridge Press, 1984.

Oe, Kenzaburo. *Hiroshima Noto [Hiroshima Notes]*. Tokyo: Iwanami Shoten, 1965.

Toyota, Seishi, ed. *Kashū Hiroshima [Tanka Anthology: Hiroshima Atomic Bomb]*. Tokyo: Daini-shobo, 1954.

Toyota, Seishi, ed. *Hankaku-shuka-hyakuzetsu [Anti-nuclear Tanka Anthology]*. Tokyo: Tanka-koron-sha, 1985.

DR. JIRO NAKANO

Dr. Jiro Nakano
currently is Director of the
International Division of Kobe
Kaisei Hospital, in Kobe,
Japan. He was a Professor of
Pharmacology at the Universi-
ty of Oklahoma and Clinical
Associate Professor of Medi-
cine at the University of
Hawai'i School of Medicine.
While teaching and maintaining his private prac-
tice in Hilo, Hawai'i, he was active in writing tanka
in Japanese and haiku in English, and contributed
to Japanese and American magazines and anthol-
ogies. In Hilo, he was a member of the Ginu-
shisha Tanka Poetry Club and the Hilo English
Haiku Club. He has written several books on
Japanese immigrants in Hawai'i, and edited and
translated *Poets Behind Barbed Wire* (a collection
of tanka by Hawaii's Japanese Americans who
were imprisoned during World War II) which won
the 1985 American Book Award. He is currently
writing a history of tanka and haiku writing in

Hawai'i and is associated with the Choon-shisha Tanka Club in Honolulu.

Of *Outcry From the Inferno*, Nakano states: "I started this project because I cannot forget the terrible experiences of the air raids in Kobe towards the end of World War II, and the memory of the dying victims of the atomic bomb that I had witnessed just after the war. I have been compelled to translate the tanka written by them to reveal their agony and their outcry to the people of the world, pleading to abolish nuclear weapons from the earth."